Annie Forbes

Something Like Grace

Something Like Grace
published in the United Kingdom in 2025
by Mica Press & Campanula Books

https://micapress.uk | contact@micapress.uk

ISBN 978-1-869848-44-6
Copyright © Annie Forbes 2025

The right of Annie Forbes to be identified as the author of this work has been asserted by her in accordance with the Copyright, Designs and Patents Act of 1988.

All rights reserved.

For Beth

Something Like Grace

Let's address the skeleton
of a lesser spotted deer
culled at the very cusp of its maturity.

In order to be able to save them
it's important to understand
the intricate and disarming truths
of how they were first assembled.

                    In a room in Massachusetts
                    tiny and disconsolate birds.

If we lay out all the pieces
it will all make sense.

                    Don't tell me it isn't important.

Certain schools of thought
point to the existence of
some sphere of perfect holiness

                    which, from the trappings of our own
                    patently unholy state
                    we are unable to conceive of.

After the worst of it was over
the chassis was a mess
of twisted-up metal.

Articles of clothing, too
were strangely and maybe even irrevocably altered.

I was afraid, and
enamoured with myself
in equal and uncomfortable measure.

I dusted my belongings down
and walked and walked
into the fullness of my senses.

> Things we lost in the heart of it;
>   things that we are losing
>   things we will continue to lose.

Stillborn

Somebody speaks your name
and with it, your bones
shift and desiccate
like strands of burnt sugar

into the flank of the hillside. I can see you
coming and going
in the swell and ebb of starlings
breasting the sky;

in the ovalled snow
inching up and down
around its brace of stems;
in the red gape of the hawthorn.

Loosed from its wires
the high course
of dully electrified air
trembles and clings.

While under the bracken's line
an ocean of noise
rises to reclaim
the fragile beginnings of a heart.

Flight

Leaving the valley, its sunlit planes
breaking and streaming away.

Your hands, still steady
clutched to the wheel. Flashes of land and sky:
their hollow conference.

Under the length of my hair
clusters of broken vessels
bursting and blossoming through. Imperceptible
as wind-caught threads.

Before us, the shadows
of lichen-swaddled pines

fall at intervals. Familiar colours
barring the road. The spaces in between
becoming a path.

Distancing

When we
talk about things like leylines
or the mournfulness of rivers
moving and moving away
from the safety of their sources

what I'm really trying to find is – truly
what is it, that
keeps you here?

I'm curious
even after everything.

—

For me it's things like seasons.
The outline of a cup.
New potentialities
of dailiness. The fact that

no matter how suddenly
I find myself crying
I will always be able to hide it.

—

- And sometimes,
when things are really critical
I think about the presence of the ocean
up at the furthest reaches of the Orkneys.

How wild it is out there.

—

We stayed in a hotel, once.
My mother and father.
With a ribbon in my hair
and the cutlery all polished up to silver.

Just beyond the limits of that place
they found a lot of little artifacts
buried apart in the sand.

Strange and unreachable animals
fashioned from pieces of bone-
the traces of civilization.

Flints

Lifted and settled, the cradled weight
of her frame, folded with impersonal haste
into its new-made bed.

Past the static drone
of daytime television, the roar
of springtime currents — lashing the tops
of a sea of parking-lot sycamores.

Each overblown howl
sunk and silenced, glancing off the glaze
of sixteen tight-shut windows.

Waking, she twists the coverlet
into a series of shapes. Comfort in the material:
its familiar planes. The neat symmetry
of each starched pleat.

Children, clattering in time
down the chalk-scrawled length
of a village high-street. The sound of their gathering voices
distorted, as through water.

A white dog,
wrapping its bloodied mouth
around a stolen hen.

When summer came, a river sprang
out of the ground. Resuming its course
through the red dust.

Within a week, it teemed with tiny things. The silvered flints
of sun-caught minnows — hanging in jars
all along the mantel. Moving in synchronised jolts
like filings stopped and pulled.

In late July, she went to watch the men
burning back the fields in ordered shifts. Cauterised dirt
black in their wake. A staggered exodus
of animals, fleeing the flames.

Anticlockwise, they worked
steadily in
towards the center.

Sanctuary

In the depths of the afternoon
things are turning. It is not
as easy as a word like dying.

That's what the animals do –
spinning around cleanly
in earthly reversal.

The increments are harder to define
like a series of little wrenches
each one leaving less than what was there

but always a remainder
to be worried and worried down. I
love you I
loved you I

It's something to do with the light, there
or the differences in night and morning air
but sometimes the wheat that fills the outer fields
is greener than the stirrings of a song
and sometimes blue.

Absolution

Above the quarry, a rain cloud shifts.
Scoured against the sky, its body
gradually disintegrates—trailing itself out
in long wisps
which drift towards the earth
like hundreds of delicate limbs.

Blindly, it feels its way
over the desolate land.
Immune to hidden hazards —
sidestepping telegraph poles
dodging the husks of burnt-out cars,
it passes, miraculously unscathed.

Day Thoughts

Since you went away
the growing possibility of finding you
in the trickier parts of mirrors.

That big one in the hall –
the whole of its backing
stretched across with felt.
Lonely and uncomfortable to touch.

Is that where you are?

Or down in the lower corners
which, all covered
with a thing like spreading clouds
seem strangely and bitterly made
for the purpose of concealment.

Little snakes
hurry around the sides.
It was my father, who made them.
Lovely and angry-eyed
they hold you for their own.

Three Rabbits

The first no more than a smear
darkening the path. A clutch of dirt
trailed along the surface of a wall.

—

Off to one side, the spine of the second
bristled like a centipede
against the light. Its absent skull

uncoupled and dragged
inch by inch, into the depths of the hedge.

—

Still recognizable
as a rabbit, the third one rests
plump and unmarked
beside the clean stalk of a hindbone.

Only the eyes are wrong: blue as milk
they leach and spill.

Rites

And the first thing to do is always to hang the washing.
My mother and I, pinning the wet slings of sheets
slips and covers, all along the line. Just like this

they washed you, and we stood
admiring your whites. The stillness of an arm,
red-freckled. Wearing a ring.

—

We have learned to mourn
indifferently, in all the proper ways. Later the wind will blow
around the house
making the taut sheets
billow and sag.

Gorbachev's Colt

Unlikeliest of orphans. Frail as a raffia dog
with a puppet's wood head

which juts from the frame —
freakish and unwieldy.

No trace of the mother
who carried you dutifully in

from the outer fields. Picking her way
with dream-like slowness
over a whited frieze.

Only the fearful efficiency of an assistant
numbly unaware

of the storied impossibility
of your eight neat hooves.

Averting his eyes, he holds you to the camera
like some omen of things to come

although the truth is you are only an animal
and behind you the world unfolds

as might be expected: green grass, blue sky
the merciful simplicity of a building.

From Above

(i)

Somewhere around Hvalba
a whale is being flayed.

Listen — the neat zip
of its hide, tougher than blue tarpaulin
coming apart
along the spine.

And later, the inner explosion
of fingers, tapping against an eye
which does not move.

— —

Yes, I can hear it
even from the waterless heights
of a sixth floor apartment.

The breathless fragility
of perfectly balanced systems—lenses and ducts
crumpling like glass.

— —

Outwardly, the sound
is indetectable.

Still it resounds
like the vibrations of a bowl —
spiralling up

to trouble the course of the gulls
who linger in stubborn hope
over a pebbled slew
of pinks and reds.

ii)

In an entirely different country
people pass in droves

before a painting of a girl
flanked by two leopards

both of which regard her
with impossible docility.

The girl is wearing wings
which may or may not be a part of her own flesh

and one of the leopards
carries a chain in its mouth.

Multiplication

Fruit of the womb.
A shattered pomegranate
against a backdrop of black earth.

Murmuring hymns,
they lower you gently
into the velvety depths of the mud.

If it wasn't raining,
the weighted scrape of rope against mahogany
might set this entire conception alight.

The thing that grew inside of you
had a mystical aspect, undetectable
to even the most sophisticated of instruments.

To hold you and lose you in quick succession
was a bliss-tinged grief too strange to define,
like biting an apple corrupt at the core

or opening a series of Chinese boxes,
in a process charged with growing promise,
to find, at the heart, a spiraling absence.

Order

The city won't do
what I want it to.

Rootless in the dark
skyscrapers tremble and   lift
clear of the faulted world.

Three carriages along
a man in his shirtsleeves is crying
whilst others are looking away.

There are so many people
in every one of these buildings

each with their own   lone
yearnings and desires.

Although it might not seem it
there is a notable difference
between these words.

It is   something about
the difference in physiology
of shepherds and their charges.

It is   something about
the softness of wandering mothers.

Learning

Coming in, the brightness of those lights
ranged in silent rows—great swathes of fire
shimmering their way

                        to the quiet inconclusion
of the shadows in Ardale lane

was heightened, even then
by some unnameable quality of the evening air
to the perfect epitome of heartbreak.

— —

It is a lasting blueness —
                        steady as the dogs

that warm their worn-out bones
    at hunting sites, and sites for burning flesh
and the poorly lit margins
of historical advancements.

Variations of which
                        might be seen to lurk
in faded reproductions
of spaces evocative of romance.

— —

Boulevards, perhaps
                      or the borders of café squares.

— —

Or — with more useful relevance
to the purposes of our example;
some well-known minor impressionist's
most celebrated image of a street scene

in the foreground of which
   (from under a thankless litany of exhaustion)
a woman lifts her glass.

The artless precision of her movement
muddied into check
                      by something like a pall;
of terror or watered chalk.

— —

It was in similar straits
                that my father and I
sat in careful thought
in a far corner of the Eagle.

                My father was weeping then;
in such a way that only I could see
after the memory of a friend.

The reckless and impossible hope
of his own bright start
lost to a length of rope
in some bitter and long-gone corner
of the family home.

— —

Optical science suggests
that many of the capabilities of human sight
should be as preternaturally impossible
as witness accounts
of certain religious miracles.

But still my father's tears
carried on falling. Flowing freely then
over the ash-scarred surfaces of our table.

And might have been accused
               (for sake of an easier out)

of lessening his ability to protect me
from the terrible mysteries of his grief
or the curious and visibly important men
who hurried around our table.

– –

But I have never really been convinced
by such tired-out notions
as the finitude of grace

               and I was already lost –
in the details of a painting
           years and years away
from the pressures of linear time

          and something my mother had said;
about the methods some little-known ceramicist had employed
in order to fuse the skeletons
of anaesthetised mice
into a setting glaze.

Inheritance

In a haze of summer   I walked
together with my father
through an abundance of lanes.

All the air was turning green.
Together, we walked
even as the light   mottled our skin

towards the horses
who stood   as they always did
waiting for something to come.

— —

Coins of brightness   like the circled gaps
through which smoke would rise
as my father burned leaves.   Singing softly

as he pushed   each damp handful
into the drum. His father
was a runner. In photographs, he wears

a t-shirt   emblazoned
with two black horses. He was the one
who took a piece of stone

and broke it in two;
revealing chalk.   That was why
the substance of the lanes   buckled and swam.

— —

Before us the living horses
shifted on their hooves.   We offered them grass
but they would not take it.

From under the trees   they watched us go
loose-jointed, shimmering
to outlines in dust.

Intrusion

All night the storm was howling. In its wake
a clutch of deckchairs scattering the lawn
and all the rooftiles broken.

There are days
when even gravity acquires the weight
of something other. When the sight

of flowers lying limply in the dirt
is hard to bear. Beyond the wall

the sense of something moving — flickering
to nothing in the shadow of the trees.

In rooms and rented studies, I have lain
for hours, trying uselessly to grasp
the care with which a leopard shapes its tongue

to gentle an ear
and why that gentling matters. Even now
I hold the hope that you might lift me clear.

The muscles losing traction, running fluid
the way a dream unspools; like quick-tipped tar
the whole of the veranda
sticky with heat.

Relative to the swift execution of an antelope
the damage is insignificant — much of the scaffolding endures
and down in the cellar

the glasses are still cool
to touch and press.

When the weather clears further
it might even be possible to take a walk amongst the gardenias:
lifting and righting their heads.

Solace

Feeling the weary heart
feeling the weary heart
                    feeling the weary heart

          opening again

as the light falls
      as the light falls
           as the light falls
over the steady brightness of the bridges.

Some days
                    my darling
I am able to convince myself   that
                wherever you are

is a better place than here.   But
today
everything is nothing more than gentle.

Little leaves
steady against the ground. And the thought
you would have liked them.

www.ingramcontent.com/pod-product-compliance
Lightning Source LLC
Chambersburg PA
CBHW061235070526
44584CB00030B/4136